DATE DUE			
DEC 2 6			
FEB 9			
APR 27			
NOV 18			
NOV 2 1 1989			

Bio   Wilson, Charles
Ger

Geronimo

GERONIMO

By Charles Morrow Wilson

DILLON PRESS, INC.
MINNEAPOLIS, MINNESOTA

©1973 by Dillon Press, Inc. All rights reserved
Fourth printing 1977

Dillon Press, Inc., 500 South Third Street
Minneapolis, Minnesota 55415

Printed in the United States of America

Library of Congress Cataloging in Publication Data

Wilson, Charles Morrow, 1905-
  Geronimo.

  (The Story of an American Indian)
  SUMMARY: A biography of Apache Indian chief
Geronimo, who rose to leadership through the ranks
and led one of the last great Indian uprisings.
  1. Geronimo, Apache chief, 1829-1909 — Juvenile
literature. [1. Geronimo. Apache chief, 1829-1909.
2. Apache Indians — Biography. 3. Indians of North
America — Biography]
E99.A6G328   970.3 [B]   [92]   73-9513
ISBN 0-87518-059-0

ON THE COVER:
*Geronimo as photographed by Addison,
Fort Sill, Oklahoma.*

*The photographs are reproduced through
the courtesy of the Library of Congress,
National Park Service, Smithsonian
Institution, and the U. S. Army
Museum at Fort Sill, Oklahoma.*

GERONIMO

Geronimo began his life in full freedom in the rugged terrain of the Southwest. The games and activities of his youth were preparation for the challenges he would face in later years. As a war chief, Geronimo led a series of raids against Mexican and American soldiers and settlers. The Apaches both suffered and inflicted great losses in these raids. Geronimo was a first-rate tactician in guerrilla-type warfare; he provided his people strong leadership in their fight for survival as free people in a free land. He died in 1909 at the age of eighty on the Fort Sill reservation in Oklahoma.

Contents

CHAPTER I

The Yawning
One

In the year 1829, just below the headwaters of the Gila River in what is now eastern Arizona, lived an Indian tribe known as the Bedonkohes Apaches. The Bedonkohes belonged to a loosely formed Apache "nation" of tribes who lived in Arizona, New Mexico, and Mexico. At that time, however, and up until 1848, both Arizona and New Mexico were part of Mexico.

The Ojo Caliente, or Warm Springs Apaches, lived closest to the Bedonkohes, in the Gila River area. Other nearby tribes were the Nedni, Chiricahua, and White Mountain Apaches. These Apache tribes had very similar religious and social customs, and often the members of the tribes would intermarry. They were friends in peace and allies in war.

In the year 1829 a boy named Goyakla, which means "Yawning One" in Apache, was born to Taklishim and Juana of the Bedonkohes tribe. When Goyakla grew up he became known by another name, Geronimo (Spanish for Jerome) — a legend in his own lifetime, a legend that has lasted to this day.

Geronimo was the fourth child in his family, and everyone believed that he was due to have good fortune throughout his life, because four was a lucky number. Geronimo's father was the son of the famous Chief Maco, hereditary or tribal chief of the Nedni Apaches. If circumstances had been a little different, Geronimo, as a fourth child, would have succeeeded his father as chief. But when Taklishim decided to marry Juana, a Bedonkohes Apache, he had to agree to join her tribe and give up his right to the chieftainship. Nevertheless, some said that the boy Geronimo spoke and even walked as if he were a born chief. And Geronimo, proud of his father and grandfather, dreamed of the day he would be a leader of his people.

An early proof of Geronimo's good fortune was that he was handsome, like his mother. His good health showed in his hair, jet black, shoulder-length, and shining. He had hazel brown eyes that were bright and intelligent; his forehead was broad, and his face well-shaped and likable. He was to grow straight and strong to a height of five feet eight inches, which was taller than many Apaches.

Geronimo was also fortunate in having a very fine memory that reached almost back to his *tsoch* — the Apache word for "cradle." In fact, Geronimo's memory served him well in later years, when he agreed to have his life story written down in English so that the white people could hear about his life from his own words. Geronimo told his story to a young Indian named Asa Daklugie, son of Geronimo's boyhood friend Juh. Asa then translated Geronimo's words into English for Samuel M. Barrett, an Oklahoma school superintendent, who wrote them down and published the book. Geronimo's vivid memory helped him describe his early life and his many exciting adventures with interesting details and deep feeling.

Samuel Barrett, Geronimo, and Asa Daklugie
working on Geronimo's life story

Geronimo remembered how as a toddler he played freely in the sun and wind and in the welcoming shade of the pines and shudock (wild cherry) trees. He recalled going out with the other children to find and bring home special treats to eat, like wild berries, sweet acorns, and richly flavored piyoñe nuts.

The open countryside was Geronimo's first school, and his parents were his first teachers. Juana, his mother, was well-known for her wisdom and skill as a mother and homemaker. She served as a midwife (one who helps with the birth of babies) and as a maker of herbal medicines. She was also known for her fine beads-and-leather work and her ability to make beautiful clothing of deerhide and other animal skins. Juana liked visiting with the other Apache tribes. When he was barely five, Geronimo made his first long cross-country walk at his mother's side, covering about four hundred miles in only nine days. Most of the way was across desert. On that trip the five-year-old learned to locate water holes by "reading" the colors of the grass, which grew greener near water.

Juana also taught her children the many legends of the Apaches, the stories of the stars and sun and clouds and how they came to be. She taught them to worship Usen, the god of the Apaches, and how to sing their prayers to him every day, asking him to make them wise, brave, and loyal. As a deeply religious woman, Juana taught that the Apache god was a father to all Apaches. He expected his children to be loyal to their tribe, to obey and respect their chief, their parents, and the tribal elders, to help the sick, the old, and the crippled, and to share with those poorer than they. Geronimo learned from Juana his strong belief in Usen and his love for Usen's people, the Apaches. He expressed this belief later in his autobiography:

> When Usen created the Apaches He also created their homes in the West. He gave to them such grain, fruits, and game as they needed to eat. . . . He gave them a pleasant climate, and all they needed for clothing and shelter was at hand. . . . When the Apaches are taken from these homes they sicken and die.

When Geronimo was only six, his father taught him to hunt on horseback without using saddle or bridle. These lessons began with riding down small game, such as rabbit or wild turkey, and striking it with a long stick or wooden shaft. In this way he learned how to use a spear. Next he learned to hunt antelope and deer, on foot and with a bow and arrow, hiding among bushes or behind trees or in the prairie grass, so he could take the game by ambush.

Learning to hunt taught him other useful skills, too. Because some of the hunting was done at night, and still more at first daybreak, Geronimo learned to walk and run in the dark. He could move rapidly for great distances and locate the creeks or springs or ground holes which supplied the water that all game animals must have.

The Apaches believed that skillful hunting was a boy's best way to manhood and to the great honor of being a warrior. Geronimo had to master the use of the three most important Apache weapons, the knife, the spear, and the bow and arrow. A good hunter had to be a good runner, a quick-witted wrestler, and a first-rate horseman. Long before he came into his teens, Geronimo was all of these.

His parents also taught him how to farm. When he was six Geronimo joined his parents and his older brother and sisters at planting, cultivating, and harvesting their *milpa,* or garden-sized field, which covered about two acres. Each family had its own milpa, usually in the valley lands where there was better soil. All the milpas were grouped in this way and usually were a mile or more away from the village of wigwams. The Apache villages were almost always at least partly hidden in mountains or forests.

Instead of plows the Apaches used big wooden hoes, which they usually made at home. Corn or maize was the most important crop. Working together, the Apache families dug the valley lands deep and planted corn in arrow-

Geronimo as an adult with his family
in their melon patch at Fort Sill, 1895

straight rows. Between the hills or clusters of corn they usually planted beans and, in the more moist places, pumpkin and other squashes and sweet melons much like our cantaloupes. When dry weather came, as it often did, they carried water to the fields in clay pots to save their crops.

Since many mouths had to be fed from the small fields, the harvesting had to be done with great care. Geronimo and his brothers and sisters helped with the harvests. As a reward for good work they were permitted to join in eating the sweet melons. When the beans and the squashes were ripe, the entire family shelled the beans and sliced the squashes for drying, first in the sun, then in baskets that were hung from the top poles inside the wigwams.

They gave even greater care to the corn. When it ripened they pulled the ears from the stalks, husked them, and for several days left the many-colored kernels to dry in the sun. Then they braided the husks together in garlands or "ropes" and carried them home either on their shoulders or by horseback. There they shelled the corn and placed the kernels in bags which they stored in caves or caverns beyond reach of the straying animals.

The work of grinding the corn into meal suitable for making thin pancakes which they called tortillas, or for loaf bread, usually fell to the women and girls. The usual way was to sprinkle a layer of the kernels on a flat stone and gently crush it with a rounded stone shaped somewhat like a rolling pin. The woman or girl knelt to do the work. There was a great deal of it. For a large family, two or three hours of the corn crushing was required every morning. Careful homemakers sieved or sifted the meal with sieves made of stiff dry grass or reeds. They usually fried the tortillas on iron skillets and sometimes made small loaves of bread which were roasted in hot ashes topped with live coals. At the time the Apaches did not have stoves. Their cooking was by frying, using animal fat as grease, or roasting in shallow pits or on open fires.

Apaches were a very hard-working people, and at least nine-tenths of all their work was to provide food for themselves. Besides farming, the children and grownups spent many hours and days finding and making use of edible wild plants. Even in the dry lands of the Southwest there were many of these. Near the rivers or creeks they found plants that bear tubers which look and taste somewhat like Irish or white potatoes. The one they liked best is now known as the Jerusalem artichoke, which has a blossom like a small sunflower.

During the summer the women and children joined in gathering and drying the various kinds of wild plums, grapes, and berries. Their favorite wild berries included blackberries, a kind of small blueberry, and a wild currant still known as the buffalo berry. This small bright red berry tastes like a sweet grape. It dries well and makes a tasty red sauce that looks like cranberry sauce but is much sweeter. The Apaches also made a candy of buffalo berries and frequently carried the sweet red chunks of candy on their travels.

Picking the wild berries had its dangers as well as its pleasures. The berries usually grew on thorny or briary plants in hard-to-reach places. Geronimo remembered berrying as a source of many adventures. On one trip he and his older brother, Perico, joined a group led by a woman named Chokole. Since the children were all very young, Chokole decided to ride her little horse and later use it for helping to carry home the berries. She also took along her dog to give warning against unfriendly berry-pickers such as bears.

After the children had scattered to search, the dog barked loudly at a large black bear which came charging through the bushes. Chokole's horse bolted, throwing its rider in front of the big black bear. The bear struck the woman's shoulder with its giant paw and broke it, then gave her a very bad head wound. But Chokole managed to get to her feet, draw the knife she carried in her skirt top, and stab the bear with enough force to drive it away. At that point she fainted from loss of blood.

After a time the children became aware that Chokole was missing. Geronimo and his brother began searching for her. They found her horse and it led them back to the unconscious woman. The boys managed to dress her wounds and to lift her back on her horse, and so carried her home. The boys had given first aid to her wounds and then called the tribe's medicine men who were expert in caring for the injured. This experience taught Geronimo to respect the fierceness of bears and the bravery of women. He would later see Apache women serving with war parties and fighting other enemies even more dangerous than large black bears.

Hunting was usually the most dangerous and exciting part of the food gathering. Most of its danger came from mountain lions or cougars that hunted the same game animals the Apaches sought. These big catlike animals usually made their homes or dens in bluffs or in hiding places near the rivers and springs where the game animals came to drink. Quite often the mountain lions would leap down on the hunter, who in order to live had to strike back quickly with his spear or knife since he rarely had time to bring his bow and arrow into use.

From time to time even the most skillful hunters would suffer flesh wounds or severe scratches, and usually they had to tend and treat their own wounds. This called for some knowledge of first aid. Hunters learned how to dress their own wounds with various kinds of molds and clay or with wild-growing plants with medicinal values. They also had to learn to use their knives skillfully to pry or cut out arrowheads or thorns that sometimes became imbedded in their flesh.

All the many hunting skills proved useful whether in war or peace. During Geronimo's youth the Apaches were at peace most of the time. But hunger was never very far away, and war was always possible.

Before he grew into his teens Geronimo had learned how to make good use of the game he killed. He learned how to dress and skin the deer, how to slice the fresh venison into thin strips and smoke-dry it over open fires and wrap the cured meat in leaves. By storing the smoked venison in cool caves it would stay good for many weeks, often several months. He also learned to cure the hides, first by soaking them in a mixture of wood ashes and water to remove the hair and soften the skin or leather. Then he stretched the skin on a wigwam side to dry, later to be used for making warm clothing.

But the bison was "king" of the game. The Apache hunters would ride after the big animal until they tired it. Then, still on horseback, they would raise a wooden lance with its head made of sharpened flint rock, and stab the bison over its heart. The meat from one bison was about a thousand pounds, or at least ten times the weight of a young boy. After the hunters brought home a bison and the people had feasted on the fine fresh meat, which tastes much like tender beef, the rest of the meat would be sliced and dried and stored with other food-stuffs in a nearby cave. The hide of a bison was valuable, too; it was cured and used to make tepees and to provide warm bedding. Hides were also valuable as items of trade; a number of them would be considered payment for a horse.

Geronimo's hunting training stressed that game should never be killed except when needed for food and leather or hide or fur. All young Apaches were taught to avoid needless killing. They were taught not to kill buffalo, deer, or other game during spring and summer when the wildlife feeds and cares for its young. The Apaches did not build fences to keep the grazing game animals, such as deer, antelope, and buffalo, from their natural pastures.

The untiring work of growing, hunting, and gathering food had rewards other than just eating the food. In the autumn of each year, after the crops were harvested and the main early autumn hunting season was over, the Apaches celebrated a great tribal feast which they called a "grand rally." Grand rallies lasted four days. Usually a tribe would be the guest of another tribe one year and would be the host to that tribe the following year. Entire villages, including men, women, children, and the aged and crippled who were able to walk, would travel overland, on foot, for a week or more to attend.

Geronimo enjoyed these feasting days very much. They were a time to make dozens of Apache friends, to meet kinfolk from other tribes, and to listen to wise chiefs, both tribal chiefs and war chiefs. A tribal chief inherited his chieftainship by birth; a war chief had to earn, by brave deeds, the right to be called chief.

As Geronimo knew, a war chief did more than make war or lead his comrades in battles. He was also a kind of local judge and police chief elected by the members of the tribe. The war chief's duties included settling arguments or quarrels among neighbors, protecting the tribe from out-laws or horse thieves, and helping his people to worship and strengthen their religious life.

Each feast day would begin with group worship. Sometimes this was an hour or two of silent prayer. More frequently it was led by an elderly man or woman who spoke and prayed for all present and directed the prayer songs in which each worshipper hummed or chanted while "thinking out" his or her own special prayer.

Geronimo's father had explained, "Prayer is better than punishment for keeping people good." He pointed out that Apaches had no jails and very little crime of any kind. A person who did commit a serious offense could be tried before his chief and tribal council. If he was found guilty he would be sentenced to banishment from the tribe, the most dreaded punishment of all.

Following the worship period, all present joined in a visiting and friendship hour. Then the women and girls prepared and served a great outdoor picnic that took place directly after noon. When all had eaten the dancing began. The music was mostly vocal; the men led the singing, or more accurately, the humming, since most Apache songs had no words. The dance beat was provided by drums called *esadadednes;* they were made of deerskin strung tightly over wooden hoops.

Games followed the dancing. For the men and boys there were foot races and bareback horse racing, jumping and spear-throwing contests, archery or bow and arrow matches, and wrestling bouts. For all present there were lively hide-and-seek games. Supper was made from the leftovers of the picnic.

Early the following May, a few weeks before his thirteenth birthday, Geronimo was faced with the saddest happening of his young life. His father was stricken with a burning fever which the medicine men, all eight of them working together, could not cure. His father died.

For the first time in his life, Geronimo felt the weight of overpowering grief. He loved his father, knew him as his finest friend. All the tribe grieved for the beloved Taklishim.

But following the burial in a secret cave, Apache custom had to be observed. It was grim and hard. In the presence of the tribal council of elder warriors and the chief, the dead man's wigwam and all his belongings were burned and his horses were turned free. Juana, Geronimo's mother, was without a home. The grieving widow did not choose to marry again. In this case, however, Geronimo, as the fourth child, asked to support and care for his mother. His brothers and sisters and other kin joined in building and furnishing a new wigwam for Juana and in making ready a new milpa for her to plant and harvest from. So Geronimo, at twelve, took over the support of his mother for the rest of her lifetime. He provided the bison skins for covering the new wigwam, tended his mother's milpa, and supplied her with meat and clothing.

By the time Geronimo was seventeen he had learned to be an excellent farmer and one of the best hunters in his tribe. In that year he took more than forty bison and almost as many deer, enough to supply his own family as well as many of the neighbors. He cured enough bison hides to buy the beginning of his own herd of horses. These small horses, bred from the once wild mustangs of the Southwest, were the only livestock the Apaches raised, and they were looked on with special pride. Frequently a man's success was measured by the number of horses he owned. Geronimo's twenty-two horses were the start of a fine herd.

One day in June of 1846, when Geronimo was seventeen, he decided it was time to speak to speak to the father of a young girl named Alope about his and Alope's wish to be married. The two had grown up together, and as long as either could remember, they had planned to be man and wife. Alope was a very pretty young woman, and many young men of the tribe were eager to take her in marriage. Also, Alope was Noposo's only daughter and she cooked and kept house for him, so he wasn't anxious to part with her.

Therefore, Geronimo wasn't surprised when Noposo set a high bride-price for Alope — a herd of thirty horses. Geronimo already had twenty-two horses, and he was sure he could persuade some of his friends to sell him eight more "on credit." One of Geronimo's many friends, the young chief Mangas Coloradas, offered, as was the custom, to speak to Noposo on behalf of Geronimo, assuring him that Geronimo would be a fine son-in-law. Noposo told Mangas Coloradas that he liked Geronimo. He was only waiting, he said, for Geronimo to bring the herd of thirty horses; then Alope was free to go with Geronimo to his wigwam.

Noposo had only a few days to wait. As Geronimo later recalled, "In a few days I appeared before Noposo's wigwam with the herd of ponies and took with me Alope. This was all the marriage ceremony necessary in our tribe."

CHAPTER II

Young Man
of Peace

Although Geronimo early learned many skills
that were to help him become an exceptional warrior and
tribal leader, he was always a peace-loving youth. He
aimed for excellence as a hunter, scout, horseback rider —
because he knew he would need those skills. But in his
early years he didn't fight or quarrel or strive for glory as
a warrior.

In fact, in Geronimo's time most Apaches were peaceful
farmers, hunters, and traders. What they called their "war
parties" were often really exploring trips, group visits,
shopping and swapping trips, or prospecting for future
homesites.

Geronimo spent much of his time exploring. From his
early hunting expeditions, he became acquainted with a
far-reaching stretch of what is now called the Great Southwest. Usually alone, he had already explored great areas
of the ragged mountains and boulder-strewn foothills. He
had learned the whereabouts of several summits where he
could look out over many miles of the dry open plains. He
explored the precious rivers and creeks and knew the
locations of many of the life-saving water holes.

It is not known exactly how far the boy roamed alone.

It is known that in company with his strong-spirited mother he had traveled and visited fellow Apaches as far away as the Chiricahua Mountains. In that Apache settlement he met and formed a close and longtime friendship with a distantly related, adventurous youngster named Juh, whom Geronimo chose to call Whoa. In boyhood Geronimo learned of many of the lands to the west of the Gila Valley. He may even have glimpsed the towering Sierra Madre, the two-mile-high range that separates the great Mexican states of Sonora and Chihuahua.

The teenage explorer certainly became familiar with many of the landmark mountain ranges. He mastered the knack of moving rapidly at night and of avoiding water sources during daytime, when there would be a danger of ambush by people or attack from animals such as mountain lions. He realized early that the best leader is the one who avoids unnecessary risks, who can learn and use more than just one route from one place to another, and who knows that a well-planned advance must include a practical path of retreat.

As a youth and as a young married man, one who was qualified to be a warrior and a member of the tribal council, Geronimo both taught and practiced peace. His marriage only added to this love of peaceful ways. It inspired him to hunt farther and more expertly than ever before and to work harder at farming. He was delighted to find that his bride was an expert homemaker and could put the pelts, hides, and furs he brought her to good use, making clothing and bedding. "Alope made many little decorations of beads . . . and drew many pictures on the walls of our home," he later recalled fondly.

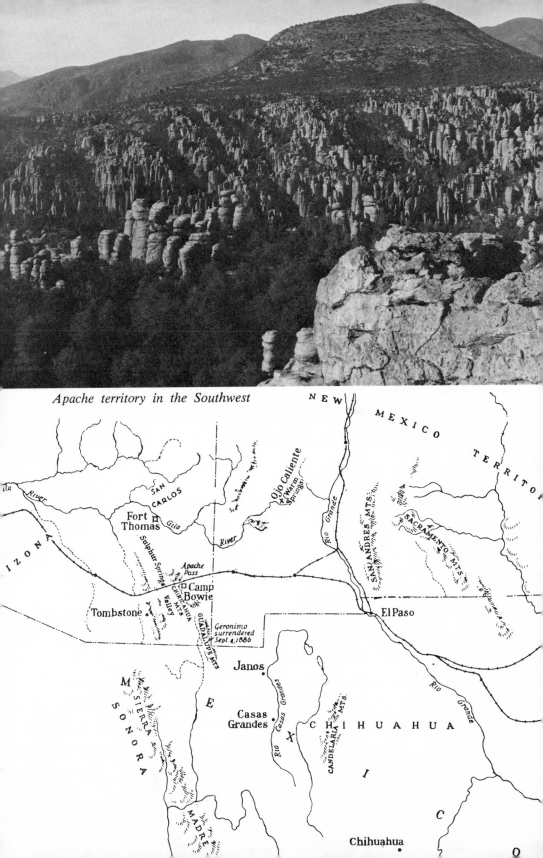

Apache territory in the Southwest

NEW MEXICO TERRITORY

SAN CARLOS

Ojo Caliente (Warm Springs)

Fort Thomas

Gila River

SAN ANDRES MTS.

SACRAMENTO MTS.

Rio Grande

Sulphur Springs

Apache Pass

ARIZONA

Camp Bowie

Tombstone

CHIRICAHUA

Valley

GUADALUPE MTS

Geronimo surrendered Sept 4, 1886

El Paso

Janos

Casas Grandes

Rio Casas Grandes

CANDELARIA MTS.

CHIHUAHUA

Rio Grande

MEXICO

SONORA

SIERRA MADRE

Chihuahua

Peaceful and happy years followed. Geronimo continued to make many friendships in his native community and beyond. Among his closer friends was his exciting young kinsman, Juh, who presently chose to join the Bedon-kohes and to court and marry one of their pretty girls who was Alope's best friend.

The two young couples were very close friends. Juh showed his adventurous nature by recommending a long, bold trading trip far down into Mexico, beyond the mighty Sierra Madre. Juh had also gone exploring, and had traveled as far as Mexico, where he had visited Apache kin and seen many Mexican villages and ranches. He pointed out that the Mexicans were well established as traders. They had many stores and trading posts and operated great numbers of mule or burro trains to haul goods from place to place.

Juh freely admitted that the Mexicans also had many soldiers, some of whom were unfriendly to Apaches, calling them "wild Indians" who always caused trouble. However, it was Juh's understanding that the soldiers and people in the Mexican state called Sonora were the unfriendly ones. Visiting Apaches could pick their way through the great mountains, traveling the valleys or plains only at night, until they reached the villages and trading camps in the more friendly state of Chihuahua.

Juh's bold plan had many good points. It would require a large force of warriors, including scouts and sentries, but volunteers could be taken from other Apache villages and tribes. The hunting had been good; the Apaches already had large quantities of pelts and furs that they could swap with the Mexicans for bolts of cloth and blankets, knives and iron hoes and other metal wares, even muskets and bullet lead and the magic exploding powder.

It would be a very long trip, granted, requiring fully a year of travel and trading. Since it would be a mission of peace, quite probably the warriors would wish to take their wives and families along. The preparations would require time, perhaps several years. But the plan was good and in time the tribal council might be convinced. Certainly the mission would benefit the Apaches and bring them closer together.

Geronimo agreed. But he recognized that the plan would need time to grow in the minds of the people and be accepted. He himself was in no hurry; he was enjoying life very much just then. By the end of their first year of marriage Alope bore a child, a daughter whom the proud young father called Juanita, perhaps in some part to honor his mother, but also to show his appreciation of Spanish names. The Apache's was never a written language, and the way it was spoken often differed from place to place and speaker to speaker. This caused some confusion not only to many white people, but also to the different groups of Apaches, most of whom also spoke a little bit of Spanish. The following year, when Alope presented him with a son, Geronimo named him Roberto. Two years later his third child, a second son, was born. Geronimo apparently put off naming his second son until the boy developed a character to which he could fit just the right name. But, as events turned out, this was never to happen.

Meanwhile, plans for the long and ambitious trading journey were taking shape. When Geronimo and Juh presented their plan to Chief Mangas Coloradas, he was deeply interested. After recommending the possibility first to the council of the Bedonkohes, he then took it to the neighboring Apache tribes. More than a hundred warriors volunteered; in time this number was doubled. The majority voted to take their families along and to muster their most capable warriors to serve as scouts and sentries.

Geronimo was delighted to find himself included among this select group. By then he was coming into the prime of his young manhood. By the following June of 1858, when the great journey was scheduled to begin, he would be twenty-nine, a twelve-year member of the tribal council and therefore a senior warrior. Although not yet a famed fighter, he was known as a thoughtful and careful planner and a master of defensive tactics, which he had learned from his big-game hunting. Geronimo was a great believer in fine old Apache proverbs; one of his favorites was: "The Apache's best friends are not his relatives but his brain, his eyes, and his hands."

Even so, Geronimo felt great loyalty for his relatives. On the trading journey he decided to take along his mother and his wife and their three young children. He knew they would be in good company. Many other wives and children were joining the great expedition of which Mangas Colo-radas would be chief-in-command. The principal party would travel on foot. Women and children, including those carrying babies or very young brothers and sisters, using the Apache "trot-walk," would average at least forty miles per day. They would also join in the night travel, keeping in touch with one another by means of prearranged bird calls. In event of attack or other danger, all would be assigned to hiding places that the scouts would select as the procession moved along. All those arrangements reflected the Apache travel motto, "Hope for the best and prepare for the worst."

The great journey began under fair June skies. The travelers took along only a few scouting ponies, one report said thirty, which did double duty by carrying large bundles of furs and pelts. Most of the girls and women carried their own fancy handiwork, mostly beadwork and tooled deerskin garments, plus a few clothes for themselves and the children. They hoped to barter their fancy goods for calico, thread, and beads. During the journey, their responsibilities included cooking, making camp, and as need be, collecting medicinal plants en route. None tried to carry more than a three-day supply of food, which was mainly smoked or dried meats. Hunters and gatherers of edible wild plants planned to keep sharp-eyed and busy as they traveled.

Chief Mangas Coloradas and some of his senior warriors were concerned about rumors that many Mexicans were unfriendly toward Apaches. The treaty which ended the Mexican War included a passage pledging the United States army to aid the Mexican army in protecting the white citizens of both countries from Indians. To the Indians this agreement was threatening, because at the time Indians were not being permitted citizenship in either country. Nothing at all had been said about protecting peaceful Indians from warlike or criminal white people. Mangas Coloradas reminded his people that wherever and however Indians traveled they should not look on white people as their friends.

At the time Geronimo did not feel great concern. He accepted Juh's word that some of the Mexicans, particularly those in Chihuahua, where they were headed, were not unfriendly toward Apaches. He was confident that by good scouting the party could avoid any possible trouble with the soldiers in Sonora. And he believed that, no matter where they were, a peaceful group like theirs would be treated as such and left alone in peace. One thing he did not understand was that, unlike Apaches and other Indians whose warriors were organized on a tribal basis, the Mexican soldiers operated as a centrally organized national army, and could therefore be moved freely across state boundaries.

The first mission, that of scouting and choosing the route, was managed skillfully. Geronimo found his earlier travels of great value. With Juh as a companion scout he easily led the way to other Apache settlements, including the Nednis, his father's people, and so across the hot and rocky San Simon Valley and into the rugged Chiricahua Mountains.

There the travelers stopped to visit the tall and splendid Cochise, the most renowned and beloved of the Apache chieftains. At each stop the travelers were welcomed and feasted and joined by new and eager followers. Happy in many friendships, both longtime and new, Geronimo listened eagerly to informed advice and welcomed new scouts into his patrol group.

The great peaceful party moved along through the far-flung, unsettled border lands into the dry, rough foothills of the Sierra Madre. Travel was enormously difficult, as the route went along steep ravines unmarked by trails of

any kind. Often water holes were fully a hundred miles or two hard days of tramping apart. After crossing well into Mexico, Mangas Coloradas assigned a large patrol of warriors to safeguard the west flank along which Mexican soldiers from Sonora might make a surprise attack. But for the time none came.

Now traveling mostly by night, the party headed into Chihuahua for Casas Grandes, an ancient Indian capital city. Two and a half centuries earlier, Spanish colonizers had built a fortress settlement near Casas Grandes called Janos, one of a line of frontier forts extending to El Paso. The dread of Indian invasion from the north was very old.

However, by 1858, the Janos settlement was believed to be peaceful. The village had stores that invited Indian trade and a large well from which Indians and other travelers were permitted to draw water. The throng of Apaches drank from the well, then pitched camp nearby and sent a party of warriors to speak for peace and explain their desire to trade. The spokesmen were cordially received by the *alcalde* or mayor, and by the merchants and other citizens, who treated each warrior with a bag of meal, explaining that their fellow campers would be similarly welcomed. The welcoming committee then presented the callers with some *mescal,* a very strong liquor made from the agave plant, with extra supplies to take with them back to their camp.

Next day a group of about forty or perhaps fifty Apache warriors went into the village to trade; they carried their barter goods but no weapons. Geronimo was one of this group. Other warriors went out to hunt game. Wisely, Chief Mangas Coloradas left a force of about twenty warriors to guard the camp, where all women and children were instructed to wait. But unwisely, he also left the mescal behind with the sentries.

The trading party spent the whole day in the village, trading as friends with the local storekeepers. They exchanged bead-and-leather dress goods and furs and pelts for sugar, salt, ready-made garments, axes, and knives. As they traded goods, the townspeople continued to treat the Indians to the strong Mexican liquor, mescal. All drank happily and perhaps too much.

That night their happiness abruptly faded. As they walked toward the camp, a group of women ran out from hiding to reveal the terrible news. During the afternoon a large band of Mexican soldiers had approached unseen, or at least before the sentries, most of whom were drunk, had recognized them. The soldiers and their Mexican Indian scouts completely surrounded the camp, loaded muskets, and opened fire, killing everyone in sight, men and women, children and babies.

Fully a hundred were slain in cold blood. The ground was littered with corpses. Only a few of the warriors had escaped. The attackers had burned all bows or spears in sight and stolen the pack animals. The hunters had not yet returned, but the soldiers were in hiding nearby, waiting to massacre both the hunters and the trading party.

In deep distress Geronimo walked across the ruined camp. One after another he found the bodies of his loved ones, first his wife, then his mother, and then all three children. He realized he had lost everything. His grief was too great for words.

At first he took for granted that the villagers, even while pretending friendship, had sent in the soldiers, because he thought mistakenly that each village or town directed its own force of warriors. The truth was that the attacking troops were part of the militia maintained by the neighboring state of Sonora, and personally commanded by the governor of that state. With the aid of Indian scouts, the Sonora force, which far outnumbered the Apaches, had been trailing the peaceful traders for several days and had surrounded their well-hidden camp to await their chance.

Mangas Coloradas took command, and confirmed that the regiment of Mexican troops was still nearby and preparing to destroy the Apaches who survived. Quickly the chief gave commands. All Apaches would leave the camp immediately. They would not take time to bury their dead; under the circumstances this would be too dangerous. They would take only time enough to care for the wounded whom they would carry away as best they could, since there was not time to build stretchers. All would move out into the darkness, trotting rapidly. They would intercept the hunting parties and head northward toward home, selecting a course that would not be easy to follow, for the Mexican soldiers and their scouts would surely be in pursuit. Most of the Apaches were now weaponless and greatly outnumbered. Their only hope for survival was in their legs, their eyes, and their wits.

Geronimo later recalled, "I had no purpose left. I finally followed the tribe silently, keeping just within hearing distance of the soft noise of the feet of the retreating Apaches. . . . I spoke to no one and no one spoke to me — there was nothing to say."

CHAPTER III

Warrior
of Vengeance

The journey home was the saddest experience Geronimo had ever known. He had lost all those he loved most and, for the first time in more than a dozen years, he was a man without a close family. He had not even been able to do his loved ones burial honors or make a prayer-wait or weep for them alone.

The long retreat was fast and successful. The Apaches were able to pick routes which not even the Mexican Indian scouts could find and to outdistance the well-equipped Mexican cavalry. But Geronimo found no comfort in the brilliance and skill of his comrades. He helped hunt, but he was not hungry. In the mountain darkness he helped find water holes for his friends, but he was not thirsty.

He found himself hungering and thirsting for but one thing, revenge. He sensed that most of the surviving warriors shared his desire for vengeance, but perhaps none so deeply as he. Apache justice demanded that the killers be killed. At that time, and for many years to come, Geronimo ceased to be a lover of peace.

Back at his Gila community, in the custom of the Apache, he burned his wigwam and his mother's and all their possessions, including his children's clothing and bedding, even their toys. Those things done, he joined a gathering of all the local warriors. The entire group and their chief and medicine men voted unanimously to take the warpath against Mexico — all of Mexico. The group also elected Geronimo to act as their spokesperson in seeking help from other Apache tribes.

Geronimo promptly set out alone for the Chiricahua Mountains and the people of the famous Chief Cochise, who welcomed him and called a tribal council for the following morning. All the resident warriors attended, seating themselves in the order of their rank as decided by age and battle experience. Geronimo waited standing until his lifelong hero Cochise bade him speak. Almost a half-century later Geronimo recalled his own words:

> Kinsmen, you have heard what the Mexicans have recently done without cause. You are my relatives . . . We are men the same as the Mexicans are. We can do to them what they have done to us . . . I will fight in the front of the battle. I only ask you to follow me to avenge this wrong.

The agreement was silent and complete. Cochise and his warriors would join on the warpath against Mexico. Geronimo resumed his lone journey, heading for the tribe of Nedni Apaches whose chief was Geronimo's longtime friend Juh.

The combined Apaches planned their strategy with great care. The three chiefs, Mangas Coloradas, Cochise, and Juh, would be joint leaders, each commanding the warriors of his own tribe. The preparations included locating and building temporary camps for all the women and children and other non-warriors, and providing them with corn, dried venison, and other foodstuffs. Apache scouts, including Geronimo, chose meeting or rendezvous places in hidden, hard-to-reach points near the boundary of Mexico and New Mexico. The Apache leaders were aware that the Mexican army would not hesitate to cross the poorly-marked boundary to attack and destroy Apache settlements in the territory of the United States. Neither did they forget the treaty that Mexico and the United States had signed, agreeing to help each fight warlike or marauding Indians.

Geronimo was chosen to lead the way into Mexico. He performed brilliantly as a scout. First he guided the women and children to the hidden camps and carefully chose spots where warriors and their dependents were to meet at a later time, as needs required. In this he was demonstrating a strategy of which he would soon be the master; it was the strategy of preparation for defeat and retreat as well as for victory and advance.

The force moved over the high rugged mountains at an untiring rate of between forty and fifty miles per day, taking great care to avoid leaving visible tracks. Once across the mountains, Geronimo began leading a series of night-time marches down the winding valley of the Sonora River, which leads into the Mexican heartland and eventually flows into the Gulf of California. As a first battle station he chose Arizpe, a former capital of Sonora and a settlement bordered by canyons that provided natural defense against surprise attack. By then Geronimo was well aware that his force was being trailed by Indian scouts employed by the Mexican army.

The Apaches had barely arrived at the old and almost vacant village when they saw a force of Mexican army scouts closing in on them. Geronimo called out the names of eight of his warrior friends and led them in luring the patrol into a nearby canyon. The Apaches then closed in from all sides and killed all of the scouts.

This, of course, was an open invitation to battle. The three chiefs joined in giving Geronimo permission to take over as war chief for the combined party; the Apaches believed in field-of-battle promotion.

The Mexican commander countered by sending forward a strong cavalry force. The Apaches took cover in gulches and thickets and struck back with a well-aimed barrage of arrows. An all-day skirmish followed in which the Mexican soldiers came out second best. The high point was the Apaches' success in capturing several Mexican supply wagons and a long line of pack mules. This provided the Indians with muskets, powder, bullet lead, and various other battle supplies. Some of the warriors were acquainted with the use of firearms, but Geronimo urged them to depend mostly on their own familiar weapons — bows, spears, and knives.

Next day the Mexicans reappeared with two companies of infantry and two of cavalry, in all about five hundred experienced combat troops, to overcome the volunteer warrior force of about one-fourth that number. The Apaches had chosen their positions with great care. When the mounted troops came closer they recognized several of the men who had taken part in the massacre of their wives and children the year before.

That was a forceful motive. Geronimo, proving his skill

Geronimo's camp in the Sierra Madre, Mexico, 1886

as a combat leader, divided his men into two columns. He directed one to open a flank attack and led the other column in a point-blank charge. The Mexican forces were off-balanced and showed confusion, finding themselves unable to effectively attack or defend. The remarkable fact was that Geronimo, who had never before taken part in a major battle, was not only leading a combat force, but by way of his truly amazing feeling for strategy and tactics, was taking the offensive against a much larger, more experienced force.

Geronimo heard two hard-pressed Apaches calling for help. He sprinted to join them, seized the spear from the fallen warrior, and faced an attacking soldier, who by then had only his cavalry saber to fight with. Geronimo ran the Mexican through with the spear, and without trying to recover it, killed another soldier with his knife and dragged his wounded companions to safety.

The baffled Mexican troops attempted to rally against the two small but mobile forces of warriors. Geronimo resumed his deadly bow and arrow marksmanship, taking advantage of cover but moving ever forward. Again and again he heard his name being called and cheered by his followers. Presently he heard the Mexican soldiers shouting his name in warning. From that day on, "Geronimo" became a famous name, honored by friends, despised by foes.

The Mexican force continued to fall back before the brilliance and fierceness of the attackers. The cavalry was unable to move effectively in the crowded canyons and gulches. The foot soldiers were out-fought and out-maneuvered at every turn. By afternoon the entire army force, its surviving scouts included, was in a confused and costly retreat. Geronimo kept up the attack until he had counted more than a hundred Mexicans dead — revenge by actual body count for the massacre of the defenseless Apaches during the previous year.

Many would recognize, as more than a few already had, that Geronimo's brilliance as a battle leader was truly historical. The victory at Arizpe was marked by a hard-to-believe flare for bold and inventive tactics which military historians and strategists continue to respect. It was and it remains a most memorable battle.

In a flush of victory, the combined Apache forces headed homeward, well armed with Mexican muskets and swords, supplied with captured food stores and blankets, and with a sizable herd of Mexican army horses and mules as additional booty. Apaches had declared war against mighty Mexico and won the first battle. Geronimo was the hero of the battle and its entire campaign.

The newly appointed war chief decided to pay a visit to the settlements of the Chiricahua tribe, mainly to see his special friend Cochise. Following his hero's welcome, Geronimo chose to stay with Cochise for awhile and build himself a wigwam. He had his own reasons. He had become acquainted with and paid courtship to Nanaga, a young woman of the village whom he found especially attractive. When he asked the chief's permission to marry her, Cochise happily granted permission and welcomed Geronimo to his tribe.

Geronimo had found some happiness again, not only in his second marriage but in the benefits that went along with his fame and success. As a war chief, by far the most renowned war chief of Apaches, he did not have to give up his membership relations with any of the tribes. As a close friend and lieutenant or aide to Cochise, he also shared in some of the honor given to this most respected of Apache chiefs.

Moreover, the Chiricahua tribe had some very important geographical advantages. The mountains from which the tribe took its name were important because they were near both Sulphur Springs Valley, a hunter's "promised land," and the Apache Pass, then the most favorable passageway from the East through the great valley and so westward to Tucson and California. Cochise's tribe held this pass, which opened on mile-high mountain summits and provided a dependable supply of water. The importance of this pass had long been recognized by Cochise, and he wanted to make sure that his people continued to control it.

Geronimo moved effectively to extend his friendships among the outlying tribes and settlements of his people. Since he was already a hero to all the Apache tribes, this was not difficult to do. But the rewards of fame did not cool his desire for continuing vengeance against the Mexican army. Geronimo was now eager to fight Mexican soldiers at any opportunity he could find, and he discussed the matter with Cochise often. Cochise clearly stated that while he did not favor another major invasion into Mexico, he was willing to permit Geronimo to make small raids at his own risk. However, Cochise stressed that the raids should be kept small.

Geronimo's first adventure was a small but extremely bold raid. "I succeeded in persuading two other warriors, Ahkochne and Kodehne, to go with me to invade the Mexican country."

The brave venture did not pay off. After crossing the Sierra de Antunez in Sonora, the fearless three were overtaken by a company of Mexican troops who opened fire and killed both Ahkochne and Kodehne. Three times the Mexicans surrounded the survivor. Three times Geronimo fought and dodged his way out. When he had shot away the last of his arrows he ran for the mountains. Mexican cavalry pursued for two days without success. But with typical frankness Geronimo listed the three-man invasion as a failure: "Having failed, it was only proper that I should remain silent." His silence lasted for several years.

In 1859, Geronimo once again led his warriors into Mexico to battle with a cavalry unit that outnumbered the Apache force at least eight to one. Taking advantage of his amazing skill at mountain-crossing, the invasion party moved over the Sierra de Sahuaripa, overtook the Mexican cavalry, slipped past it, and under Geronimo's direction set up an ambush in a mountain gulch which the troopers were obliged to follow.

This time the Mexican force fought back bravely. But the Apaches responded with their war cry and a fury of hand-to-hand combat that severely injured, then drove away the mounted troops. The Apaches also lost heavily; ten of their warriors were killed.

After burying their dead and attending the wounded, the Apaches turned home triumphantly yet heavy of heart. "In this fight we had lost so heavily that there really was no glory in our victory," Geronimo later recalled.

But the ambitious war chief continued to yearn for glory. During the following June he recruited a smaller group of twelve volunteers for another bold raid into Mexico. Far down in Chihuahua the war party captured a great train of pack mules laden with valuable merchandise. But before the Apaches could count their bounty they were overtaken by a force of Mexican soldiers. Geronimo was seriously wounded by a bullet which struck just below his left eye, leaving him partly blinded for several months. Once more the invaders were obliged to bury their dead and retreat to escape capture.

The increasing number of Apache raids resulted in more and more opposition. As the American Civil War began to flame, the United States army was forced to withdraw from the line of Indian outposts. But the Mexican army was determined to make the Apaches pay, and they marked them for total destruction. Mexican commanders and governors started to shift to the offensive by invading Apache homelands. The Mexicans were recruiting more Indians for scouting and patrol duties.

After Geronimo and his surviving invaders had returned to the Gila River settlements, three well-armed companies of Mexican troops moved secretly across the border and the protective mountains. The invaders waited to attack until most of the male Apaches had left for Navajo country to trade for blankets. After nightfall, they surrounded the settlement and attacked from all sides. Again they opened fire killing nine children, five women, and four of the remaining warriors.

In spite of his serious eye wound, Geronimo managed to get on his feet, put an arrow through one of the Mexican officers, and escape. But the Mexican troops burned all the wigwams, seized all arms and provisions, took away all the horses they could catch, then as a final warning and insult, took away four of the Apache women to be used as slaves.

In time three of the women managed to escape and return to their village. Geronimo was deeply impressed by their bravery. The youngest of the three escapees, a seventeen-year-old named Francisco, also had to suffer through an attack by a mountain lion one night on her flight home. The big fierce cat tore away much of the girl's left shoulder and dragged her several hundred yards. By grasping bushes Francisco managed to break free, draw her knife, which she had stolen from her captors, and stab the mountain lion. Geronimo resolved to pay more heed to the bravery and resourcefulness of women. In time women were admitted to Apache war parties. Some of them proved to be as strong and skillful in fighting as the male warriors, and when they did, the men treated them with the respect they deserved.

Meanwhile the latest Mexican raid left the entire Gila settlement in an almost desperate plight. It faced the oncoming winter without food or housing. Geronimo and his warrior followers helped rebuild the ruined wigwams and replenish the food supplies, principally with venison and the edible wild plants. But none of the food sources was plentiful. Winter brought hunger and cries of children in more than one Apache camp. And the Mexican raids continued.

CHAPTER IV

The Master
Raider

While the Union and Confederate armies were fighting each other elsewhere during America's Civil War, Mexico's federal and state troops struck harder and harder against the Apaches. More and more wigwams were being left charred and smoking. More and more hidden caverns were being used as Apache cemeteries. More and more children, wives, and mothers were in mourning.

An important result of the far-ranging Mexican attacks was to bring the Apache tribes closer together than ever before. Once more Apache chiefs agreed that their best defense was to take up the offensive. Geronimo heartily agreed. He pointed out, however, that with so many Apaches suffering from hunger, it was important for their offensive to serve two purposes. First, it should carry the thrust of warfare back into Mexico; secondly, the war parties, with the same risk and effort, should be able to return with badly needed food and other necessary goods.

In the early fall of 1862 Geronimo set out to provide a demonstration. At his native village he carefully selected eight warriors and led them afoot toward Mexico. After five days of what he termed "mountain trotting," he and his followers located a trader's trail in the Sierra de

Sahuaripa well in Mexican territory. The invaders set up a well-hidden camp and waited. Early next morning four horsemen came in view leading a long line of pack mules weighed down with bulging loads of blankets, saddles, bolt cloth, tinwares, and bagged sugar.

With only slight effort Geronimo and his men frightened away the riders, took over the entire mule train, and headed it toward home. Across the border at San Catalina the raiders met another mule train loaded with nothing but cheese, tons and tons of it. Like most other people the Apaches loved cheese. Perhaps never before had nine warriors come home with such a huge quantity of cheese.

Mangas Coloradas welcomed the homecomers and assembled the entire tribe for an all-night celebration. As Geronimo described it, "We gave a feast, divided the spoils, and danced all night."

Geronimo's party expected to be pursued by Mexican troops. Mangas Coloradas called out his warriors to serve in a combat patrol which he invited Geronimo to lead. By moving out quickly the patrol located two companies of pursuers. The horseless Apaches completely destroyed both the Mexican cavalry company and the Indian-Mexican infantry. The fighting was difficult but nobody could deny the total brilliance of Geronimo's leadership. The war chief recalled only: "For a long time we had plenty of provisions, plenty of blankets, and plenty of clothing. We also had plenty of cheese . . . ."

The raids were continued. For the most part they were successful. But unfortunately the need for more raids increased, because natural resources that had sustained the Apaches for generations were disappearing. The bison and the deer, foremost suppliers of meat, leather, and coverings for wigwams, were growing scarcer. A succession of dry spells was reducing the yields of the garden fields. As a good but primitive people the Apaches were more and more defenseless against the changing world around them.

Geronimo's moral standards were distinctively Apache. He accepted that he and his people were children of nature, and as such were entitled to the products of nature, including food and self-made lodging. His concept of property rights was based on the idea that what one needed one should have. If the gifts of nature were withheld, if food supplies and the open range and other necessities of life were seized and hoarded by others, the Apache was entitled to seize or otherwise retake them. The tribe and the tribal settlement were the only political and social groups he understood and recognized. On this basis he saw Mexico as a very large tribe that chose to make war against his own much smaller tribe. He believed it his duty to resist and strike back. Thus, the raids, as he saw them, were just.

In the early autumn of 1864 Geronimo carefully planned a special cavalry raid. He chose twenty volunteer warriors, providing each with a fast and sturdy horse and a supply of bows and arrows and spears. Then he moved the rest of the Gila River Apaches and some of the neighbors to distant and securely hidden camps, so that they would be safeguarded against return raids by the Mexican soldiers.

Geronimo led his mounted warriors south, below Tombstone, Arizona, and into the huge Mexican state of Sonora. First the warriors raided several Mexican villages, avoiding bloodshed, and, as Geronimo noted, "securing plenty of provisions and supplies." Near Pontoco the raiders captured another mule train. Its cargo included baskets filled with many bottles of the strong liquor called mescal. The warriors began drinking and several fights broke out. When Geronimo ordered these ended, he was not obeyed. When he mustered a night watch to guard the camp from probable attack by Mexican troops, his orders were again disobeyed; the sentries kept on drinking.

For the first time Geronimo faced the fact that liquor was one of the worst enemies of his people. "My warriors were too drunk to walk. . . ," he recalled. "I poured out all the mescal and put out all the fires." He also treated the wounds of several of his warriors who had been injured in the drinking brawl. Next morning he led a "head-achy" return to Arizona. On the way the party was able to seize a herd of cattle. The raiding force returned to the hide-out camps, escorted their tribespeople home, divided the spoils, and joined in a feast.

But not all the raids were so successful. During the following year, 1865, Geronimo and nine followers were attacked by a large force of Mexican soldiers, who forced them to scatter and abandon their "liftings." Geronimo paid them back the following year when he led a force of thirty warriors all the way to Santa Cruz. This raid proved successful. The captured goods included a very large herd of cattle and an additional herd of pack horses that were almost hidden under their huge bundles of loot. While returning from their thousand-mile sweep, the Apaches proved to be superior cattle drivers and horse handlers as well as successful raiders. The negative side was that, for the first time, they indulged in violence. The warriors killed civilians as well as soldiers; reportedly at least fifty Mexicans, for the most part civilians, met death at the hands of the raiders.

Clearly the raiders were beginning to see the Mexicans as mortal enemies as well as an important source of what their leader termed "provisions and supplies." Clearly, too, the unique leadership of Geronimo had grown to be a prime ingredient of successful raiding. When the son of Chief Mangas chose to repeat Geronimo's success by leading a group of eight mounted warriors himself, he was surprised by a Mexican cavalry force and came out second best. Geronimo, who went along as one of the volunteer warriors, later explained, "I was always glad to fight the Mexicans. But [this time] we arrived home . . . with no victory to report, no spoils to divide, and not even the ponies we had ridden into Mexico. The expedition was considered disgraceful."

Not surprisingly, Geronimo moved quickly to erase the disgrace. He chose five particularly able warriors and, traveling afoot and at night, proceeded to the area of Arizpe in Sonora. There his group carried out a series of highly successful night raids on prosperous cattle ranches.

But this was not the end of it. Several of the *rancheros* organized their own cowboy combat group or posse and rode into Arizona, into the mountain country near the Gila River Apache settlement. There the invaders waited until the Apache warriors left on a long hunting trip, then attacked the village, recovered their cattle, and took away all the Apaches' horses. Again Geronimo moved quickly, recruited a force of twenty experienced warriors, trailed down the Mexican ranchers and their cowboys and recovered most of the horses and cattle. The bold leader assigned three of his followers the job of driving home the recovered livestock and led the rest in what might be called a "super-raid." This daring night raid was carried out so skillfully that the rancheros and their men woke to find the rest of their on-trail horses and cattle had mysteriously vanished.

Geronimo described it as a "great joke." But the shaping events were not in the nature of a joke.

Geronimo on the right
with three of his warriors

CHAPTER V

Apache Chief

The confused and confusing ending of the Civil War was throwing strange shadows on the far-flung South-west frontiers. A new generation of white settlers, many of them young, poor war veterans, was in a pioneering mood. But mixed up with these basically law-abiding citizens were a number of "bad guys." These included gangs of smugglers who made a business of carrying goods across boundaries without paying duties, cattle rustlers, and gunmen out for hire.

Travelers were being robbed and murdered. Frontier homes and new settlements were being looted and destroyed. Sheriffs, judges, and other officers of the law were constantly being made the victims of the outlaws. And all the while, Apache raiders were being accused of these crimes, though they were not guilty.

Like many of his fellow Apaches, Geronimo was quite aware of the unjust charges made against them. He insisted that at their most violent he and his raiders never behaved as the professional outlaws did. They fought as warriors; they did not slay women and children or judges or priests or the white medicine men.

He recognized that the many changes going on around

them were affecting his people. On all sides white settlers were homesteading or otherwise taking over what had been Apache farmlands and game ranges. The remarkable tools known to white people as plows were digging and scraping away the green-grassed valleys. Game was no longer plentiful. Wild-growing berries, nuts, and other edible plants and numerous medicinal plants were growing scarcer, some even disappearing completely.

For the most part the Apaches showed or felt no special dislike toward the newly arriving white people. As Geronimo would later explain:

> We could not understand them (the white people, including the migrant land surveyors) very well, for we had no interpreters. We made treaties with them by shaking hands and promising to be brothers. We traded with them. We also brought them game, for which they gave us some money, We did not know the value of this money, but we kept it and later learned from the Navajos that it was valuable.

Geronimo and his people knew that the Mexican government was doing little to control or oppose the rapidly increasing gangs of outlaws, who included Indians as well as white men. Instead, Mexico was, in effect, declaring war against all Apaches, whether residents of Mexico or the United States. As the 1870s began, the Mexican government continued to harden its stand. Repeatedly, attack parties of Mexican troops moved at will into United States territories to "punish" Apache settlements. There were worrisome reports that U.S. army troops stood by to join the Mexican forces, crossing into Mexico when and if their mission so required. Both countries seemed to classify the Apache's as an "outlaw's nation."

By 1872 Geronimo and his longtime friend Juh had taken over as fellow war chiefs. By then Juh was also the senior or tribal chief of the Nedni Apaches, some few of whom were residents of Mexico. The bold, sometimes hasty Juh favored moving all Apache tribes into Mexico, where greater quantities of unclaimed lands waited. He pointed out that since the Mexican-United States boundary no longer provided any dependable protection for Apaches, the Indian nation would do best to make a final stand within Mexico.

Geronimo was not wholly convinced of the long-term correctness of such a move, but he was willing to try it out. He strongly favored replacing the now-and-then raids with open battles between Apache warriors and the Mexican armies.

A test maneuver is remembered as the Battle of White Hill. There Geronimo led a charge of sixty warriors, afoot and armed with only bows and arrows, spears, and knives, and wholly destroyed two well-armed Mexican cavalry companies, although the Mexicans fought bravely.

The subsequent fights showed there were many good warriors among the Mexicans. Geronimo became convinced that the resettlement of all Apache tribes on more plentiful lands south of the border was simply not possible. The effectiveness of the Mexican troops was rapidly improving as both the federal and state governments of Mexico began using increasing numbers of Indian scouts and matching infantry forces with cavalry.

As the 1870s wore on, the Gila River Apaches, to whom Geronimo had again returned, and the more numerous Nednis, with Juh as their senior chief, were supplying most of the volunteer warriors. Geronimo remained the vigorous symbol of the fighting genius of an Apache warrior. He was the unrivalled master of exact timing, placement of forces, strategic use of land surface, and of darkness and hand-to-hand combat. He was also a brilliant student of the strengths and weaknesses of his foes. Within the same hour he could be, and frequently was, a gracious companion, an effective persuader, a master diplomat, and an untiring warrior. He could keep his war parties in effective action when outnumbered as many as a hundred to one. He freely admitted, however, that he could not accomplish miracles — such as overcoming the combined Indian-fighting soldiers of the two foremost powers of North America.

During the year 1883, after months of almost continuous skirmishing with overwhelmingly large forces, Geronimo put aside all hopes of resettling Apaches in Mexico. The Apache-style warfare, which would become known as guerrilla tactics, had grown to be his prime interest and concentration. He was aware that his fame was spreading like morning sunlight.

During his fifty-fifth birth month — June, 1884 — Geronimo returned to his native village to recruit some of the younger Bedonkohes as warriors. He made reunion there with his second wife and the young son she had borne him. He saw in this son, whom he named Robbie, the makings of another able warrior. The boy was handsome and nimble and growing tall.

But the great war against the whole of Mexico was

calling out to him. With the attack force he had recruited, Geronimo went south where he knew that thousands of Mexican troops waited in hopes of destroying him. Once more at Arizpe he settled his handful of warriors in a rugged canyon and joined them in scraping out some shallow trenches. He had already sighted the scouts of a Mexican combat regiment.

Next he found where the general of the regiment was and eavesdropped while the general lectured his officers. "Officers, in those ditches is that red devil Geronimo and his hated band. This must be his last day. . . . Dead Indians are what we want."

Thankful that he understood Spanish, Geronimo responded by carefully aiming an arrow that killed the general. Then he hurried back to his men to make them ready for the mass attack that was sure to come. As the companies of soldiers moved through a crescent of tall dry grass, a detail of Geronimo's warriors slipped behind them and set fire to the grass. In the heat and smoke and fiery confusion all the Apaches managed to escape. The soldiers were unable to pursue them effectively. Geronimo and his warriors picked their way back home to Arizona.

As another winter settled in, Geronimo took time to consider the situation. It was obviously changing for the worse. He realized that his people were growing ever poorer. The game was vanishing. White settlers kept pouring in on them like a winter's snowstorm, settling the open lands, taking over the precious springs and water holes.

As the green pastures grew smaller, so did the head counts of Apaches. Smallpox and fevers were taking their tolls. In many places hunger was weakening a once strong

Geronimo on horseback

people. All Apaches could not be supported by a succession of loot-acquiring raids. Even all the Apaches together could not fight and conquer the entire Mexican army. Geronimo reflected that he had never bothered to count all the Mexican soldiers he had killed. But he could count his own battle wounds, eight of them, including a Mexican musket ball that remained in his right leg.

Added to the problem was the fact that United States soldiers were arriving in ever greater numbers. Again and again he heard reports that they were joining the Mexican troops to destroy the Apaches. Many years earlier, beginning in 1863, as Geronimo knew, the white chiefs in a distant town called Washington had urged all Apaches to cease invading Mexico and stay closely in their ancestral homelands. The advice had largely been ignored.

However, one respected chief showed signs of interest. Mangas Coloradas, with an escort of three warriors, had personally answered an invitation to journey to an outpost settlement called Apache Tego, in New Mexico, to meet with officials of the United States. The proposal he heard was that, in return for peacefully moving his tribe to that area, the white people's government would reward them with beef, blankets, meal, and other necessities. It was practically an order for the Gila River tribe to agree to a confinement on lands actually foreign to them. Geronimo saw no merit in the proposal and emphatically opposed it. Mangas Coloradas put the decision to his tribal council. The votes for and against going to the reservation were about even. For the most part the aged and the cautious were in favor.

After lengthy discussion and argument Mangas Coloradas, by then an old man, led a group of about a hundred Gila River Apaches to the reservation in New Mexico. It was not a joyous leave-taking. Obviously it further reduced the already small numbers of Gila River Apaches, and weakened their ability to defend themselves against Mexican soldiers and their Indian scouts. The smaller numbers would also reduce the effectiveness of community farming and hunting. And, Geronimo clearly saw, the division of the Gila River tribe left those who stayed more dependent than ever on the food and other necessities obtained through raids.

For a long period, the tribe waited for news of the Apaches who had chosen to accept the "invitation" of the white government. Here the faults of the Apache communications system showed up. Lacking a written language and a postal service, the Apaches could not exchange letters. Naturally, most of the tribespeople were hesitant to visit the reservations kept by the government of the white people, who were not yet proved or dependable friends.

So the Apaches had to depend on rumors or reports from passing travelers. These reports were anything but good. The word presently "leaked" that the Apaches were being betrayed in New Mexico, and that the white soldiers had killed Mangas Coloradas. Deeply worried, the Bedonkohes met in council and voted to make Geronimo their senior tribal chief as well as their war chief.

This, of course, was a high honor. But it added to Geronimo's numerous problems. Already the highest-ranking war chief, he depended on at least two of the other tribes for warriors. And as he was already waging war against the whole of Mexico, he could not sanely declare war on the whole of the United States by attempting a rescue of his tribespeople who had been taken over by the United States government. He was well aware that the duties of a senior chief, as opposed to a war chief, consisted primarily of attending to the everyday needs of the tribe. Obviously he could not properly attend all these responsibilities while leading war parties to and from Mexico. He therefore believed that he could contribute most by continuing his raids, thereby helping sustain his people, while the tribe's elders took charge of the home settlement.

Then, news of the tragic fate of Mangas Coloradas arrived at the Bedonkohes camp. When Mangas reported to the reservation, the old chief had been placed under custody in an army guardhouse. Sentries were ordered to shoot him down if he tried to escape. That night someone threw a rock through the guardhouse window, striking Mangas in the chest. The old chief cried out in pain and got to his feet. At that moment several sentries shot him down in cold blood. Gruesome insult was added when an army doctor performed an autopsy and dispatched the old chief's skull to the Smithsonian Institution in Washington as an "exhibit."

Mangas Coloradas' people were very bitter now, and Geronimo began leading raids again with increased vigor. Between raids, Geronimo worked towards another important goal: bringing the Apache tribes closer together. As a first move he led his home tribe on a group visit to the lands of the Warm Springs Apaches in New Mexico. There all were cordially welcomed by Chief Victorio and his Ojo Calientes. Geronimo later summarized: "When we had stayed as long as we should and again assembled some supplies we decided to leave Victorio's band. I do not think we ever spent a more pleasant time."

Unfortunately much of what followed was less pleasant. As the troops of both the United States and Mexico continued to join forces against him, Geronimo was forced to accept the fact that he could not indefinitely sustain his people by means of the raids. When a party of Indian scouts came to the Gila River settlement and invited him to meet their commander or white chieftain, Geronimo went with them.

At Fort Bowie near Apache Pass, Geronimo met the American general, O. O. Howard. General Howard explained that his president, or Great White Chief, had sent him to make peace with the Apaches, or, at least, to "offer" peace. The offer included supplying all Apaches with government issues of needed food supplies and clothing, as well as providing twelve head of beef cattle each month for each band or settlement. All this as a reward for living at peace seemed attractive enough. Geronimo was favorably impressed by General Howard. But he was afraid that, as the saying goes, there were "strings attached." These, of course, included being confined on reservations, probably to be guarded by white soldiers. Geronimo explained that he would require time to ponder the offer and discuss it with his people.

After returning to Gila River, he found many worsening problems. For one, outlawed Apaches, those who had been banished by their tribes as punishment for serious crimes, like abandoning families and disobeying a chief's orders, were organizing raiding gangs of their own. The gangs were robbing trading posts, stores, and nearby white settlements. There were growing numbers of family quarrels and petty feuds among warriors. The deepening poverty of the Apaches was behind much of this discontent. Hunting was becoming worse and worse. Repeated droughts, or dry spells, were withering the garden fields and changing once green valleys to desolate brown. Apache communities were beginning to break apart. In some cases poverty-stricken families sought refuge individually on the government reservations. Some had slipped away to the San Carlos reservation in New Mexico. Others were moving out quietly with plans to join the Apache tribes in Mexico. Geronimo decided to lead what remained of his village to Warm Springs where they continued their visit with Victorio and his tribe.

The following year was quite a happy one. Geronimo was able to resume his much interrupted family life. His third wife, a Nedni woman called Lenna, gave birth to a very pretty girl baby whom the proud father named Eva. Geronimo's second wife had died of a strange and fierce fever which the wisest of the medicine men could not cure. But his son Robbie had survived the fever and was strong and well. By then in his middle teens, Robbie was proving his skill as a hunter and was on his way toward qualifying as a warrior.

CHAPTER VI

Betrayal

One day during the time Geronimo and his tribe were still visiting Victorio, a large party of Indian scouts employed by the U.S. Army arrived at the Warm Springs settlement. Geronimo was concerned by the number of the scouts; two fully armed companies were arriving, enough to do battle effectively. But the leader of the scouts insisted that they came as friends, with a peaceful invitation. Their mission was to persuade the two great Apache chiefs, Geronimo and Victorio, to come with them to a friendly meeting with the leaders of the American army.

The two chiefs decided to accept the invitation, but Geronimo paused long enough to recruit an escort of seven able warriors. Even so, the Indian scouts had the Apaches outnumbered better than ten to one.

It was a very odd welcome. On arrival at the army headquarters all the Apaches were stripped of their weapons, arrested, and thrown in the guardhouse. They were told that they were to be "court-marshalled." At the time Geronimo and his friends did not know the meaning of that word; they did know it couldn't be good. Next day Chief Victorio was released. But Geronimo and his escort warriors were held in the army prison for four painful months.

Finally they were tried by a board of army officers, and released on their solemn promise to lead or otherwise move the remaining Bedonkohes to the reservation. Geronimo kept his promise and managed to persuade the remainder of his tribe to follow him to what he could only think of as an outdoor prison.

For two years he and his people lived on the reservation peacefully, if not happily, for there were several disturbing developments. Word reached them that Chief Victorio, "the Good One," had been slain in cold blood by soldiers when he protested the forcible removal of his tribe to the reservation. That, of course, was a sad and completely unjust ending to an exceptionally good life.

There were other injustices, too. Only a small part of the promised foodstuffs and other supplies were actually delivered to the Apaches on reservations. Not even the beef steers were being delivered as promised. There was no doubt that several of the government suppliers were dishonest.

The threat of imprisonment lingered. The resettled Apaches tried very hard to be self-supporting. Again they grew corn and beans and squash and tried to hunt game, although the land was poor for both farming and hunting. There was much sickness, and all longed for their freedom.

Rumors were their only contact with the "free world" they had earlier known. Again the rumors were bad; it was said that the American army planned to permanently imprison all the Apache leaders and perhaps the warriors as well. One day a party of army scouts arrived to inform Geronimo that he and an escort of his warriors were to meet a group of army leaders at Fort Thomas, another new outpost on the Gila River. Later Geronimo explained, "We did not believe any good could come of the meeting . . . so we held a council ourselves and fearing treachery, decided to leave the reservation. We thought it more manly to die on the warpath than be killed in prison."

The decision was a bold one. With Juh at his side, Geronimo and his followers, about 250 of them in all, set out across wild country to Mexico. The White Mountain Apaches were able to supply the refugees with some rifles and ammunition.

For an entire year they managed to live in that area of wild rough mountains. When extreme hunger and cold set in, they raided American farms and ranches. But the suffering was great and there was no real solution. The wandering Apaches voted to return to Arizona and try to locate a new homeland there.

Naiche and Geronimo
at Fort Bowie, Arizona, 1886

On the way Geronimo learned that army scouts had orders to arrest him and to kill him if he resisted. He set out alone on a bold tour to recruit additional warriors. At about this time, his lifelong friend and fellow war chief Juh died in Mexico from an accidental fall off his horse. The valiant warrior Naiche, son of Cochise, replaced him as chief of the Nedni Apaches. Geronimo, however, remained an important and respected war leader. As such he continued to recruit an adequate force of followers.

When he had enlarged his band to about four hundred possible combatants, including several brave women who volunteered to serve as warriors, the group joined in his decision to return to Mexico. They could not locate any suitable living place in Arizona.

This time U. S. troops, principally Indian scouts, reinforced by a like force of the Mexican army, followed relentlessly. In the foothills of the mighty Sierra Madre, the combined scouting force attacked the well-hidden Apache camp. Again most of the casualties were women and children.

As he led his surviving followers up into the higher mountains, Geronimo learned from his own scouts that General Crook and several companies of U. S. troops were in Mexico to aid in capturing or destroying all the Apache survivors. With a heavy heart, Geronimo saw his hopes of settling in Mexico fading. While setting up a hideout camp in the Sierra de Antunez, he was visited by one of General Crook's scouts who came unarmed and alone. The scout told him that General Crook waited to meet him as a friend, and Geronimo decided he would talk with him.

When the two leaders met, the general did not mince words. He asked Geronimo to bring all his followers back to the reservation in New Mexico. Further fighting was senseless. If they remained in Mexico Geronimo and his followers would surely be trapped and destroyed. On the reservation all would be protected and fed by the United States. Another army leader, General Nelson A. Miles, was taking command of all the army posts of the Southwest. Miles was known to be sympathetic toward Indians.

Geronimo called his followers together. For the moment at least, they voted to permit the U. S. troops to lead them northward, but to do so only as an escort force, not as captors. But for reasons best known to the Apaches, the group mind changed abruptly. On the first night, the Apaches slipped out of the camp and vanished into the nearby mountains.

Council between Geronimo and General Crook,
who is wearing the white pith helmet, 1886

Both armies gave chase, but the Apaches could move more rapidly than even the best mounted troops. They kept to gulches and along precipices which no sizable body of troops could follow, not even the Indian scouts.

The escape turned out to be a contest of fleetness and endurance. The soldiers stayed in unrelenting pursuit. Without food supplies Geronimo and his warriors resumed their raids with desperate intensity.

From time to time the Apaches paused to strike back at their pursuers. But this was of little or no avail. In a wild high chasm Geronimo found himself facing another scout from the United States forces. He brought the message that the American president would guarantee peace and safety to all Apaches who would return to American soil and pledge to live peacefully. Would Geronimo be willing to give such an assurance to the new white army chief, General Miles?

Geronimo stated his own willingness and assembled his followers for council. All were in agreement. With an escort of warriors, the great war chief followed his brother to the general's headquarters. There he directed his warriors to form a line facing a line of Miles' soldiers. "We placed a large stone on a blanket before us. Our treaty would last until the stone crumbled to dust." All the Apaches gave over their weapons. "I will quit the warpath and live in peace hereafter," Geronimo promised.

General Miles stooped and cleared a bit of ground with his hand. "Your past deeds will be wiped out like this and you will start a new life."

The date was September 4, 1886.

CHAPTER VII

The Sad Years

While speaking his oath of peace, Geronimo had no way of knowing what was taking place in the high councils of the white people's government in Washington. For example, he could not know that the Senate of the United States, on February 11, 1887, had passed a resolution directing General Miles, then commanding the "Department" of Arizona, to "vigorously destroy or capture all hostile Apaches." Meanwhile the War Department had issued an order to its troop commanders to "chase and destroy" all Apaches, hostile or otherwise.

Unquestionably, every hand in the War Department was turned against the Apache. This department of the federal government had repeatedly condemned the faults and viciousness of Apaches, but it never mentioned Apache bravery or the brilliance of their fighting tactics against overwhelming odds. The War Department did not recognize, for example, the fact that on many of his raids into Mexico, Geronimo and his warriors had stood against forces that outnumbered them many times over, and had superior weapons as well. Geronimo's talent for surprise attacks and guerrilla warfare earned him an impressive military record, yet this was not taken into account.

More important, the War Department had not publicly recognized the real motivations behind the Apaches' actions—that they did what they must to survive. Nor did they consider how their ability as warriors and raiders might be converted to peaceful and useful ends. One senator from the state of Arkansas pointed out on the floor of the Senate that fully half of his fellow lawmakers had never even seen an Indian, could not recognize any one of the many languages of these first Americans, and did not know the Indians were granted no status or constitutional rights as a citizen, either state or federal, although many Indians had fought for the the United States in each of the nation's major wars.

What Geronimo did not know, but soon came to realize, was that his oath of peace and his acceptance of peace terms would make him, all his warriors, and all his people prisoners of war in custody of the United States.

Some part of the less-than-honest misunderstanding may have been due to the confusion of languages. George Wratton, a former employee of the U. S. government, was the only interpreter. As usual, Wratton had to translate English to Spanish, which some of the Apaches understood, and then the Spanish to the language of the Apaches.

The basic fact remained: Apaches were indeed prisoners of war. Geronimo and his followers were herded together, disarmed and searched, and headed northward toward New Mexico and the reservation site. A minor change of government plans caused the Apaches to be taken directly to a compound or stockade at Fort Bowie. They were herded overland much in the manner of cattle, except for the fact that their "drivers" were heavily armed.

Although Geronimo was guarded with very special care, he was permitted to ride his small horse, a spirited "dun" —a brownish-gray horse with a white face and white lower legs, or "stockings," and a gift for responding to whistled signals and various bird calls which Apaches used as passwords. This favor was not a recognition of rank. The famed war chief had lately suffered a broken arm which had not healed well.

At Fort Bowie the group was divided and the plans were changed again. Geronimo and eight of his senior warriors were chained and shackled and hauled in army wagons

Apaches and guards
en route to prison in Florida

to San Antonio, the nearest railroad station. Still in chains and heavily guarded, they were loaded on a train and taken to the prison at Fort Pickens, near Pensacola, Florida. There Geronimo and his comrades were used as convicts, put to sawing logs and similar hard labor.

The rest of the captive tribespeople were also shipped off to a prison in Florida, to Fort Marion and the old prison fortress that faces the sea in the St. Augustine area. The choice of locations could hardly have been worse. The wet, warm Florida climate was a most troublesome change from the dry, cool climate of the far Southwest highlands. Sickness flared up, fierce malaria and severe dysentery.

Without trial the Apaches had been convicted and sentenced. The first "term" covered two years. Until May, 1887, Geronimo was not even permitted to see his kin and tribespeople. There were no published records of the number of Apaches that died in prison. It is known, however, that 386 Apaches were delivered at Fort Bowie, and the proportion of prison deaths was appallingly high. After the first twenty-four months, only 166 of the original group were living. Almost 200 had died during the first period of imprisonment—well over half of the original total.

The surviving Apaches were next moved to an army prison camp or stockade near Vermont, Alabama. There for five more terrible years the group lived as prison inmates. The food was bad, the living quarters terrible, the climate deadly to Apaches. Disease was not the only killer. Two veteran warriors managed to kill their wives, then themselves. The second death toll reached fifty-six.

"I looked in vain for General Miles to send me to the

land (reservation) of which he had spoken. I longed in vain for the implements, house and livestock promised me," Geronimo recalled.

The sad years continued into 1894, Geronimo's sixty-fifth year. During 1892 he had managed to get his third wife, his surviving daughter Eva, his daughter-in-law, and his grandchild temporarily transferred to the Mescalero Indian Agency in New Mexico. He loved all of them dearly, and felt lonely without them, but he felt life would be better for them there. He believed that all that lay before him and his followers was death in the dreary prison.

But late in 1894 a long delayed glimmer of hope became visible. The prisoners heard a rumor that Washington had at last decided to move the surviving Apaches from prison to a reservation. Word came that the new home of Apaches would be somewhere in the western part of the Indian Territory, which is now part of the state of Oklahoma. More exactly, the new Apache reservation would be in the rolling drylands near another army outpost called Fort Sill.

Many questions were left unanswered but at least there was hope that some part of the promises made many years earlier by General Miles would be honored. While waiting the next move, Geronimo began to give much thought and study to the mysterious ways of the "Powers of Washington." By gradual stages he became convinced that General Miles, and, for that matter, Generals Howard and Crook and perhaps other army leaders, had intended and even tried to keep their promises. But there had been government men above them who had stopped them from keeping their word. He would presently find out a great deal more.

The new Apache homeland was not the kind of settlement site that most white Americans would yearn for. Most of the earlier white settlers had passed it by. Many had described it as "good country to starve in." Even so, the Fort Sill countryside was far, far better than the hot, dank prison stockades in Florida.

Along a sleepy little river called Cache Creek the land was usually dry but could be farmed. Each Apache family would be permitted to make use of ten acres of the valley land. They could also range livestock on the nearby grazing lands, which, although rough and boulder-strewn, were grass-bearing at least part of the time. The government's Indian Bureau would provide the Apaches with a few cattle, pigs, chickens, and turkeys.

The Apaches wished to make cattle their principal livestock; they were not very interested in chickens or turkeys and had no interest at all in pigs, since they had never eaten pork. And as was their custom, the Apaches wished to grow corn as their main food crop. But the reservation commanders, who were young inexperienced army officers, insisted that they plant at least half of their field land to kafir and sorghum, grains something like corn that grew well on dry land. Experience soon proved that the Cache Creek lands were not suited to crops that the Apaches had earlier grown and preferred.

Nevertheless, all tried very hard to adapt themselves. They dug catch basins to hold the rainwater for their livestock. They built temporary homes, either log shacks or wigwams covered with secondhand army tenting. They cleared trails and narrow roadways to join their shelters into villages. They gladly received the government issue of a few breeding cattle, even though these were rather scrubby and lean. They were delighted to receive a new "start" of the small hardy mustangs which they called ponies.

But the Apaches continued to meet many problems. For one, the new land was too hard to till with hoes. It required plowing and the Apaches had never used plows. When the Indian Bureau provided plows, they were much too large for their little horses to pull effectively. By a silly mistake, the harnesses provided were also far too big for the little horses; the ponies could almost walk through collars that had been made for giant draft horses.

With much hard work, and by gradual, painful stages, the Apaches learned how to live as farmers, at least partly self-supporting. The achievement turned out to be another lifesaver. The government "contractors" or suppliers were often dishonest, and again and again the promised supplies failed to arrive. Entire herds of cattle mysteriously disappeared en route to the reservation. When the Apaches were at last able to raise their own cattle, with a surplus to sell, half of the money they received was taken over by the "post commanders" and placed in a so-called Apache Fund.

No Apache ever saw any part of this fund. Geronimo complained in vain to five successive post commanders, all young army officers. When he told the last of these that he intended to report the holdout to "Washington," young Lieutenant Purington answered, "I don't care if you do. You and your red trash are only convicts."

Fortunately, some of the soldier guards, particularly the enlisted personnel, were kind and gracious. The same was true of some of the Indian Bureau personnel. But the good men of both services seemed unable to work effectively together. Much of the time the soldiers did not know what the civilian employees were trying to do, and vice versa. And many of the suppliers were untrustworthy. Within a year the promised issues of clothing and blankets had ceased completely.

Meanwhile the Apaches worked on, growing more and more self-sufficient. As the years crowded on him, Geronimo worked harder than he had ever worked before. Once more he began to find a little happiness. He was being true to his promise to keep the peace.

CHAPTER VIII

A New Century

Geronimo was seventy-one when the new century began, and the new century was to bring many changes. Geronimo himself, most famous of Apache war leaders, was changing to an effective peace leader. One reason for this was Geronimo's acceptance of a new religion.

At the small and somewhat homely Fort Sill Mission the aging chief had heard of a strange and wonderful prophet, who was, he said, "a mighty medicine man of the spirit"— Jesus, the Christ, who called himself the Son of God.

"I have always prayed," Geronimo explained, "and I believe that the Almighty has always protected me. Since my life as a prisoner began, I have heard the teachings of the white man's religion and in many respects I believe it is better than the religion of my fathers."

Thoughtfully and by his own free choice Geronimo was self-converted to Christianity. During the summer of 1903 he quietly joined and received baptism in the Dutch Reformed Church. He regarded that as one of his wisest decisions. "I have advised all my people who are not Christians to study that religion because it seems to me the best religion for enabling one to live right."

Geronimo also stated that the other most special blessing

of his old age was the companionship and presence of his surviving daughter, Eva. He had been grateful when Eva, at age eleven, was returned to him from the mission. Beautiful and winsome as a child, she was nearing an even more lovely womanhood.

At seventy-five the old chief sought again to provide his daughter with a mother. By then Eva's own mother had died, probably of tuberculosis. Without even mentioning his last wife's name, he later explained with typical frankness, "We could not live happily together and separated. She went back to her people. This is an Apache divorce."

But he still had his lovely daughter. And the remarkable series of adventures that was Geronimo's life still had more surprises ahead for him.

Thanks to General Miles and by special permission of Theodore Roosevelt, a friend of the Indians who was then President of the United States, Geronimo was permitted to attend the St. Louis World's Fair, more formally named the Centennial Exposition Commemorating the Louisiana Purchase. Although he had to go in company of guards, he found it a wondrous experience.

"I am glad I went," Geronimo said in his autobiography. "I saw many interesting things and learned much of the white people. They are kind and peaceful. During all the time I was at the fair no one tried to harm me in any way."

But there was one more high point to come in Geronimo's lifetime, the coming-out party for his daughter Eva. It would be a true Apache fiesta and celebration. In 1905, directly before the first September full moon, Geronimo passed the word to all Apaches and the neighborly Kiowas that his daughter Eva had "attained womanhood." He was therefore calling for an appropriate coming-out party and dance in recognition of the fact that his daughter was putting away her childhood and becoming a woman.

The announcement and open invitation came as no real surprise. Eva was pretty and charming and she already had suitors, among whom one Johnny Kee was thought to be the most favored. The festivities would last two days and two moonlit nights — "on the green on the south bank of Medicine Creek." Geronimo, his friend Chief Naiche, and the Apache medicine men directed the festivities.

The great event opened with an outdoor feast around a central campfire. When the feasting was finished, Eva came forward alone and danced once around the camp fire. She then selected a young woman companion who joined in dancing twice around the fire, then a third companion who joined in repeating the dance three times, then a fourth who joined in dancing four times around the fire.

Next the medicine men entered, stripped to the waist with their upper bodies brightly painted, to dance the sacred dances. These were followed by some amusing clown dancers. All guests then joined hands and danced in a circle around the camp fire, loudly humming their own music. After that, any older people who wished to could retire.

Then the lovers' dance began. The men, or warriors, stood in the center of the circle, while the women, two together, danced forward and chose a warrior partner. The chosen warrior faced the two women. When they danced forward he danced backward. When the paired women danced backwards toward the outer fringes he followed, facing them.

The medicine men circulated among the dancers to keep

away the evil spirits. In time the warriors assembled again in the center of the circle. This time each woman selected a warrior as her dancing partner; naturally Eva as the bride-to-be selected her groom, Johnny Kee. At daybreak when the couples' dance ended, each warrior gave a present to the woman who had chosen him as her dancing partner. It was a truly splendid celebration.

During the following years, Geronimo found himself living alone. But his heart was still strong. He dutifully kept up with his farming and his duties as a chief. These included presiding at councils, helping care for the sick, counseling all who sought his advice, and sharing his harvests with those poorer than he.

The farming season of 1908 was a good one. Late in August as the harvests began, the aging chief led his people in prayers of thanksgiving, speaking in Apache but directing the prayers to the One he regarded as the Almighty for all.

As the long chill winter settled, Geronimo continued tending his cattle, cutting wood, and doing other chores.

Early the following February, the exact date was probably February 10, he rode alone into the crossroad village now called Cache to do some shopping. Since the weather was gloomy and bitter cold, the old chief completed his shopping and for a time warmed himself and visited with friends in the general store.

At dusk he strolled to the store porch and whistled for his horse, which did not require hitching or tethering. When the little gray responded, Geronimo bagged his purchases behind his saddle, mounted easily, and rode away into the cold wet darkness.

Geronimo at Fort Sill, 1902

About two miles from his cabin the old man, for reasons not surely known, fell from his horse into roadside weeds that were being powdered with light snow. None could recall that he had ever before fallen from a saddle. But Geronimo was eighty, and eight times wounded.

In any case he lay all night in the grass, probably unconscious, certainly alone. It was early next morning before Eva and her husband found her father's empty-saddled horse and began the search for the fallen rider.

With the help of Apache neighbors they carried Geronimo, still unconscious, to the Fort Sill Hospital. He had developed a severe pneumonia.

On February 17, he died. All the Apaches, and the neighboring Kiowas as well, were deeply grieved. A visiting missionary conducted a Christian burial service. A resident white soldier, Master Sergeant Morris Swett, asked and received permission from the tribal council to build a monument, a plain pyramid of native stone.

But all who knew him justly and well knew that Geronimo's truer monument had been built of courage, of his genius as a magnificent warrior, and of unfailing devotion to his people. In the words of his last wish, which expresses all Geronimo lived and fought for:

> There is no climate or soil . . . equal to that of Arizona. It is my land, my home, my fathers' land. . . . I want to spend my last days there, and be buried among those mountains. If this could be I might die in peace, feeling that my people . . . would increase in numbers . . . and that our name would not become extinct.

THE AUTHOR

Charles Morrow Wilson has had a long
and varied career in communications.
He has been a newspaper reporter and
correspondent for the *St. Louis Post-
Dispatch* and the *New York Times.* As a
magazine writer, at various times he was
associated with Crowell-Collier, Curtis
Publishing Company, and Reader's Digest.
He has also been a contributor to many
other magazines and reviews. Mr. Wilson
is the author of many books, including
*Backwoods America, Roots of America,
Rabble Rouser, Ambassadors in White,
Empire in Green and Gold, Tropics: World
Tomorrow, Liberia: Black Africa in
Microcosm,* and *The Commoner: William
Jennings Bryan.* In view of his accom-
plishments and contributions, it is not
surprising that Mr. Wilson received a
Distinguished Alumnus Citation from the
University of Arkansas, and a citation for
outstanding contributions to Inter-American
Relations from the University of Florida.

OTHER BIOGRAPHIES
IN THIS SERIES ARE

William Beltz
Robert Bennett
Crazy Horse
Oscar Howe
Pauline Johnson
Chief Joseph
Maria Martinez
George Morrison
Daisy Hooee Nampeyo
Michael Naranjo
Osceola
Powhatan
Red Cloud
Sacagawea
Chief Seattle
Sequoyah
Sitting Bull
Maria Tallchief
Tecumseh
Jim Thorpe
Tomo-chi-chi
Pablita Velarde
William Warren
Annie Wauneka